Hickory Dickory MATH

Teaching Math With Nursery Rhymes and Fairy Tales

by Cecilia Dinio-Durkin

SCHOLASTIC
PROFESSIONAL BOOKS

New York ❋ Toronto ❋ London ❋ Auckland ❋ Sydney

Dedication

To Pete, who has proved time and again
that fairy tales can come true
To Macallan, who is our greatest proof

Acknowledgments

A special thanks to Madeline Chang, a wonderful teacher
and friend, for her encouragement and support.

Edited by Jean Liccione

Cover design by Jaime Lucero

Cover and interior art by Theresa Fitzgerald

Interior Design by Ellen Matlach Hassell
for Boultinghouse & Boultinghouse, Inc.

ISBN: 0-590-06541-6

Contents

Introduction

Listening to nursery rhymes and fairy tales is as much a part of childhood as taking first steps and learning new words. This book brings the wonder and enchantment of those familiar rhymes and stories and connects them to a mathematical context. The activities here arise from the energy, whimsy, and fun that the rhymes and stories bring to mind, while providing a wonderful vehicle for reinforcing mathematics skills and concepts.

I've adapted some of the poems and stories to meet the needs of today's children and today's math classroom. While compiling this book, I chose poems and stories that address mathematics or that naturally lend themselves to mathematical extension. For example, children will have fun classifying all kinds of ducks including the Ugly Duckling. They'll use fractions to put Humpty Dumpty together. And they'll use estimation and counting skills as they see how many children lived with the Old Woman in the Shoe.

I hope that through the math activities I've suggested, you will be able to share with children in your classroom the excitement of first introducing, or further enhancing, the familiar images of these rhymes and tales.

Although I've included six nursery rhymes and five fairy tales in this book, there are many poems and stories still waiting for you. So please keep reading nursery rhymes and fairy tales to children— while keeping an eye out for math opportunities!

—*Cecilia Dinio-Durkin*

How to Use This Book

This book contains nursery rhymes and fairy tales complete with illustrations and fun activity suggestions for you to use to teach math. Whether the rhymes and tales are familiar or new to children, read them aloud to your class before doing the activities. Since the verses and tales do vary, you'll always have one version at hand that will be compatible with the accompanying activities.

Read Aloud, Read Along

Each nursery rhyme and fairy tale is reproduced and illustrated so that you can make class sets to distribute. These will make it easy for you to introduce each math activity through the literature. So read the poem or tale first and enjoy it with your class. Then read it again to introduce the math. Some of your better readers may chime in on the reading; others may want to take the poems and stories home for families to read aloud again and again.

Journal, Journal! Read All About It!

Some activities can be concluded by having children write or draw responses in a separate notebook or math journal. If you regularly use math journals, the Assessment Ideas section included with many activities provides questions that can be used as journal prompts. And if you do not regularly use journals in math class, here are several ways to get started.

1 The physical journal can be loose papers contained in a folder, sheets of paper folded and stapled together, or blank notebooks bought from a store. Or use the My Math Journal reproducible on page 64 of this book.

2 Math journal entries can be as simple as recording a guess before actually discovering an answer, or as complex as writing an explanation of the day's math.

3 You can have children write or draw in their journals every day, once a week, or as each new skill is learned—it's up to you. Any way you use them, journals are a valuable tool that display children's progress and give you insights into their thinking.

Math With Rhyme—And Reason

The activities that grow out of nursery rhymes and fairy tales will develop children's mathematical **problem-solving** and **reasoning** skills. You'll find ideas for helping children **communicate** about mathematics and use mathematical language and symbols. The activities also foster **connections** and help children relate math to other areas of the curriculum.

To help you use this book along with your own curriculum, the following chart lists the math curriculum standards as outlined by the National Council of Teachers of Mathematics for Grades K–4. Using the chart on page 6, you can see the mathematical focus of each activity.

MATHEMATICAL SKILLS AND ABILITIES

	One, Two, Three, and Four Legs	The Months of the Year	The Old Woman Who Lived in a Shoe	Baa, Baa, Black Sheep	Hickory Dickory Dock	Humpty Dumpty	The Ugly Duckling	Goldilocks and the Three Bears	The Three Little Pigs	Little Red Riding Hood	The Pied Piper of Hamelin
Problem Solving	Determining sequential order	Ordering months, weeks, days	Determining relationships between size and amount	Determining addends for a given sum	Telling time	Re-creating shapes	Determining likenesses and differences	Making comparisons	Determining relationships between shape and area	Meeting given conditions	Meeting given conditions
Communication	Relating words and numbers	Reading a calendar	Recording results	Using manipulatives; using number sentences	Relating words and numbers	Using fraction models	Representing with charts and graphs	Justifying answers	Using a model	Representing with number sentences	Using money models
Reasoning	Using logic	Using logic	Making generalizations	Finding number patterns	Relating time and daily activities	Using logic; following a visual model	Identifying similarities and differences	Comparing, contrasting	Drawing conclusions	Comparing	Finding number patterns
Connections	Math and Writing; Literature Links	Literature Links	Literature Links	Literature Links	Math and Writing; Literature Links	Literature Links	Math and Writing; Math and Art; Literature Links	Math and Science; Literature Links	Math and Writing; Social Studies; Literature Links	Math and Writing; Literature Links	Literature Links
Estimation			Estimating number, volume		Estimating time			Estimating size, volume, temperature	Estimating area	Estimating length	Estimating money amounts
Number Sense, Numeration	Numbering to 6; ordinal numbers	Numbering 1 to 31		Finding different addends for a given sum		Equivalent fractions; making one whole					Place value
Whole-Number Operations				Understanding addition		Addition of fractions (informal)	Addition and subtraction			Addition	
Whole-Number Computation				Adding two and three addends			Adding and subtracting to compare amounts			Adding lengths	Sums to 12; adding money
Geometry and Spatial Sense			Visualizing, comparing size			Identifying shapes; re-creating shapes from a pattern			Finding area of familiar shapes	Mapping	
Measurement		Time: days, months			Time to the hour			Size, temperature, volume	Area	Length	Money
Statistics and Probability							Making a pictograph; using a Venn diagram		Making a chart		
Fractions and Decimals						Halves, fourths, eighths					Money
Patterns and Relationships		Patterns on a calendar		Addend patterns		Relationships of halves, fourths, eighths	Sorting and classifying		Combinations		Patterns of sums

One, Two, Three, and Four Legs

Two legs sat upon three legs,
With one leg in his lap;
In comes four legs,
And runs away with one leg.

Up jumps two legs,
Runs from three legs,
Catches up to four legs,
And makes him bring back one leg.

One, Two, Three, and Four Legs

ENJOYING THE NURSERY RHYME

Read the poem to your class. Then distribute copies of the poem and ask children to identify the number words. With the help of the illustration, ask children to determine what is meant by "one leg," "two legs," "three legs," and "four legs." Reread the poem and invite children to read along.

ACTIVITY One, Two, Three, and Four

Children sequence a picture story and order from 1 to 6.

Grouping: individual

Materials: One, Two, Three, and Four Legs reproducible page 9, scissors, pencils

Here's How:

1 Give each child a copy of the One, Two, Three, and Four Legs reproducible page. Ask children to look at the pictures while you read the poem to them. Then invite children to explain what is happening in each picture.

2 Have children cut apart the pictures and rearrange them in order according to the sequence of actions described in the poem.

3 When all children have put their pictures in the correct order, tell them to number them from 1 to 6 in the square provided on each picture. Then ask several volunteers to explain to the class their reasoning for determining the order of the pictures.

4 Have children bring their numbered pages to you to check. You can then staple the pages together to make a booklet of the poem, which children can take home to share with their families.

Here's More:

Introduce the ordinal numbers *first* through *sixth* and have children write them in the rectangular boxes under each picture.

Math and Writing

❀ Have children paste or tape each picture onto a sheet of paper and copy the lines of the poem that correspond to the picture below it. For children less skilled in writing, make copies of the poem on page 7 and have children cut apart the stanzas and tape them beneath the correct picture.

❀ Write a class One, Two, Three, and Four poem and display it complete with pictures on a class bulletin board.

Literature Links

Children will have fun counting with Jane Miller's *Farm Counting Book* (Simon & Schuster, 1992) and counting back from 10 to 1 with Molly Bang in her *Ten, Nine, Eight* (Greenwillow, 1983).

One, Two, Three, and Four Legs

The Months of the Year

January brings the snow,
Makes our feet and fingers glow.
February brings the rain,
Thaws the frozen lake again.
March brings breezes, loud and shrill,
To stir the dancing daffodil.
April brings the primrose sweet,
Scatters daisies at our feet.
May brings flocks of pretty lambs,
Skipping by their fleecy dams.
June brings tulips, lilies, roses,
Fills the children's hands with posies.
Hot July brings cooling showers,
Apricots, and gillyflowers.
August brings the sheaves of corn,
Then the harvest home is born.
Warm September brings the fruit;
Owls then begin to hoot.
Fresh October brings the pheasant;
Then to gather nuts is pleasant.
Dull November brings the blast;
Then the leaves are whirling fast.
Chill December brings the sleet,
Blazing fires and Holiday treat.

The Months of the Year

ENJOYING THE NURSERY RHYME

Read the poem to your class. Invite children to talk about their own experiences with weather in various months of the year. If you live in an area that doesn't experience the seasonal variations described in the poem, you may want to explain them. Review the following vocabulary words. After you share a definition, invite children to point to the corresponding picture on the poem page.

fleecy dams soft, fluffy sheep

gillyflowers carnations or other spicy-smelling flowers

primrose a tube-shaped, bright-colored flower

sheaves tied bundles of cut stalks of wheat or other grains

pheasant a colorful, long-tailed wild bird

This would be a wonderful poem to have children memorize and perform in costume for friends and families.

ACTIVITY 1 Create a Class Calendar

Children identify and order months of the year.

Grouping: individual

Materials: Months of the Year reproducible page 12, scissors, pencils, crayons

Here's How:

1. Copy and distribute the Months of the Year reproducible page. Ask children to look at the pictures and follow along in order as you reread the description of each month from the poem page.

2. Have children cut apart the months and scatter them on their desktops. Together, name the months of the year in order and ask students to find the months as they are named. Then have children put the cards back in sequential order.

3. When children have completed the activity, read the poem once more so that they can check for accuracy. You can write the months in order on the chalkboard as another way for them to check the order of their own cards. Invite children to color their cards.

4. Staple children's sets of cards together and have them keep the booklets as a reference for the next calendar activity.

Assessment Ideas

Ask questions such as these to determine children's familiarity with the names and sequence of the months.

- Which is the first month of the year?
- Which month comes between September and November?

MATH ACTIVITY CENTER Order, Please!

Write each month on a strip of paper and put the months up on a bulletin board in the correct order. Provide a cut-apart set of the Months of the Year reproducible cards. Tell children to match each card with the correct month by pinning the card underneath the name of the month.

Literature Links

Use one of these books to reinforce understanding of the seasons: *A Year in the Country* by Douglas Florian (Greenwillow, 1989); *A Busy Year* by Leo Lionni (Knopf, 1992); *Caps, Hats, Socks, and Mittens: A Book About Four Seasons* by Louise Borden (Scholastic, 1989); *Chicken Soup with Rice* by Maurice Sendak (HarperCollins, 1962).

Name _____

The Months of the Year

ACTIVITY 2 The Days of the Month

Children identify the days of the week and numbers from 1 to 31.

Grouping: pairs

Materials: The Days of the Month reproducible page 15, pencils, crayons or markers, complete calendar for the current year

Here's How:

1 Show children various months from a calendar. Point out the days of the week. Show children that the months have different numbers of days and ask volunteers to find the last number on each calendar page. Make a chart on the chalkboard for the months that have 28, 30, and 31 days. Then read this poem to the class and review your chalkboard list:

> *Thirty days has September,*
> *April, June, and November;*
> *February has twenty-eight alone,*
> *All the rest have thirty-one,*
> *Except in leap year, when's the time,*
> *That February has twenty-nine.*

2 Divide the class into pairs. Copy The Days of the Month reproducible page 15 and label a page for each month. Write the number 1 in the correct box for the current year to designate the first day of each month. Then distribute one month to each pair of children. If you have more than 24 children, more than one pair will complete the same month. With an uneven number of children, you may want to have groups of three work together.

3 Have children take turns, each using a different color crayon or marker, to number the days of their month. Remind them to stop at 28 (or 29 if this is a leap year), 30, or 31.

4 Collect the months for reuse in Activity 3.

Assessment Ideas

Here are some sample questions to have children discuss as a class or respond to in their math journals.

✵ Did you and your partner each write the same number of days? Count them to see.

✵ How many full weeks were there in your month?

✵ What were the dates that fell on Mondays in your month?

✵ How many Saturdays were there in your month?

Literature Links

Read about a week in the life of a black-and-white cat in Cindy Ward's *Cookie's Week* (Putnam, 1992). And don't forget Eric Carle's *The Very Hungry Caterpillar* (Putnam, 1981) about a caterpillar who eats his way through the days of the week.

Here's More:

If you'd like children to remember which months have 31 days and which have 30, you can show them the "knuckle method." Tell one child to make two fists and hold them up together. Each knuckle represents a month with 31 days. The spaces between each knuckle are the months with 30 days, and February with only 28 days. Recite the months in sequence as you point to the child's knuckles or spaces. Have children take note of which months fall on the knuckles (the months with 31 days) and the months that fall in the spaces (the months with fewer than 31 days). Note: There will be one space and one knuckle left over!

ACTIVITY 3 Special Days

Children identify dates of holidays and special days.

Grouping: whole class

Materials: The Days of the Month reproducible page 15, crayons or markers

Here's How:

1 Reread The Months of the Year poem to the class. Make a class calendar by reusing children's month reproducibles and adding special days in each month. You can assign colors and ask children to designate each type of special day by outlining the date with a given color. For example:

* **Birthdays** Have each child in turn tell the date of his or her birthday. Help children find the correct month and date and outline the boxes in red.

* **Holidays** Have children tell some holidays they are familiar with, such as Thanksgiving, Valentine's Day, the Fourth of July, and so on. Help children find the correct month and date and outline the boxes in blue.

Other special days you might want to find: the beginning of the seasons, days off from school.

2 Children could share cultural holidays with the class. You may want to invite family members to tell about their own holiday traditions.

3 A computer program such as Broderbund's Print Shop Deluxe can help you make a calendar for children to take home or use in class.

Assessment Ideas

Here are sample questions for your class to answer together.

* On what day of the month is your birthday?
* How many days are left in the week (month, year)?
* How many days has it been since the beginning of the school year?

Literature Links

Books children will enjoy that highlight holidays and special days include Byrd Baylor's *I'm in Charge of Celebrations* (Scribner, 1986) and Carol Blackburn's *Waiting for Sunday* (Scholastic, 1991).

Name _____

The Days of the Month

Month: _____

Sunday	Monday	Tuesday	Wednesday	Thursday	Friday	Saturday

The Old Woman Who Lived in a Shoe

There was an old woman
Who lived in a shoe.
She had so many children
She didn't know what to do.

She gave them some broth
Without any bread,
Then kissed them all round
And sent them to bed.

16

HICKORY DICKORY MATH   SCHOLASTIC PROFESSIONAL BOOKS

The Old Woman
Who Lived in a Shoe

ENJOYING THE NURSERY RHYME

Read the rhyme aloud to your class. Ask children to imagine some other things the old woman might have done with her many, many children. Make a class list. If you wish, distribute copies of the poem for children to read, color, and take home.

ACTIVITY How Many Children?

Children use estimation and counting.

Grouping: individual

Materials: How Many Children? reproducible page 18, paper, pencils, scissors

Here's How:

1 Reread the poem. Ask children to imagine how many children could fit in the old woman's shoe house. Then invite children to guess how many "children" could fit in their own shoes!

2 Give children paper and ask them to trace the outside of their shoe onto the paper. Make one of your own as well. Have children cut out their shoes. Hold up two of noticeably different sizes and ask children to guess which shoe would hold more children. Ask volunteers to explain their reasoning. Repeat the comparison with other pairs of shoes.

3 Distribute a copy of reproducible page 18 to each child. Ask children to guess how many of these children would fit in their own shoe. Record some of their suggestions on the chalkboard. Then have children put their shoe tracing over the faces on the reproducible and retrace it. When they remove the shoe pattern, have them count how many children are inside the traced outline. Help children count and record the actual number.

4 Discuss children's answers. How close were their estimates to the actual numbers?

Here's More:

Have children guess how many counters such as bears or blocks will fill one of their shoes. After a guess, have children fill their shoes to the top with the counters. Then have them dump the counters, count them, and see how close their guess was.

Assessment Ideas

Since this is an estimation exercise, there are no wrong answers as long as children can justify their estimates. Children should improve in their ability to estimate comparatively: which will hold more and which will hold less.

Literature Links

Words such as *a lot, many, few,* and *big* are used as general estimates when we don't need to know exact numbers. *Many Is How Many* by Illa Podendorf (Children's Press, 1970) is a good book with which to introduce these comparison words to your class. In Kathy Darling's *The Jelly Bean Contest* (Garrard,1972), characters try to determine the number of jelly beans in a jar. Let children try this after you read the story to them.

How Many Children?

HICKORY DICKORY MATH   SCHOLASTIC PROFESSIONAL BOOKS

Baa, Baa, Black Sheep

Baa, Baa, Black Sheep
Have you any wool?
Yes sir, yes sir,
Three bags full.

One for my master.
One for my dame.
And one for the little girl
who lives down the lane.

Baa, baa, Black Sheep
Have you any wool?
Yes sir, yes sir,
Three bags full.

Baa, Baa, Black Sheep

ENJOYING THE NURSERY RHYME

Read the poem to your class. If sheep raising is part of daily life for any children in your class, encourage them to share what they know. If not, talk with children about why sheep are sheared: each spring the thick winter coat of fur is clipped off, and during the remainder of the year a sheep's coat grows back (much like children's hair when they get a haircut). The wool is used to make woolen yarn, which is then knit into sweaters or made into cloth for clothing, blankets, and so on.

ACTIVITY Counting Bags of Wool

Children count and find number combinations.

Grouping: pairs

Materials: Counting Bags of Wool reproducible pages 22–23, counters (10 per pair), 6 construction paper cutouts to represent sacks of wool, 3 strips of paper with the words *Master*, *Dame*, and *Little Girl*

Here's How:

1. Post the *Master*, *Dame*, and *Little Girl* strips on a bulletin board. Hold up 3 of the construction paper sacks. Recite the poem again and ask a volunteer to pin the paper sacks under the people to show how the sacks were apportioned in the poem (one to each person). Then ask the class how else the 3 sacks could have been distributed. Invite volunteers to rearrange the sacks to show each combination that is mentioned. For example, all 3 sacks could have been given to the dame; 2 could be given to the master and 1 to the little girl; and so on. Repeat the activity with 6 sacks and ask children to devise ways to show how the sacks could be distributed.

2. Divide the class into pairs and distribute reproducible pages 22 and 23 and 10 counters to each pair. Tell children to pretend that each counter is a bag of wool. From the activity sheet, read the revised poems one verse at a time to your class. Discuss how the poem has changed.

3. Have children use counters to complete the charts by putting the counters in the space below each character in the poem. Ask them to find at least two ways to show the total number of bags of wool. Then have them pick one of their ways to record in the spaces provided on the reproducible.

MATH ACTIVITY CENTER How Many Bags?

Enlarge the figures of the master, dame, and little girl on a copy machine, or make drawings of your own. Post the words to the poem on the bulletin board, leaving the quantity of bags of wool blank. On squares of paper, write numbers from 3 through 20. Provide enough counters to represent up to 20 bags of wool. Show children how to use the center by picking a number to fill in the blanks in the poem and then using counters to show the combinations of bags each person in the poem could get. Have children list their combinations.

4 For the verse on reproducible page 23, invite children to decide their own number for the total number of bags of wool. Then tell partners to come up with combinations of bags for the number they have chosen. They should draw their total number of bags of wool in the last column.

5 Call on different pairs of children to share their versions of the poem. On the chalkboard, make a class list of all the different combinations for each total. Use additional cut-out bags at the bulletin board if children need help seeing how the bags could be distributed.

Here's More:

If you haven't written equations with your class before, this is a good opportunity to start. Help children write an equation for each of the combinations they made. For example:

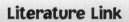

Master		Dame		Little Girl		In all
1	+	1	+	1	=	3
2	+	1	+	3	=	6

Assessment Ideas

✸ Encourage each child to show you a different combination to make a given total number. Have partners check each other for accuracy.

✸ Ask students to find the following combinations: the dame gets the greatest number of bags; the dame and the little girl get the same number of bags.

✸ With 10 bags in all, how many would the little girl get if the master got 5 bags and the dame got 4 bags?

Literature Link

To help children understand how wool is used to make clothing, read *Charlie Needs a Cloak* by Tomie de Paola (Simon & Schuster, 1973). This is a charming story about a shephard who uses the wool from his sheep to make his own shawl.

Name _____

Counting Bags of Wool

1. Baa, baa, Black Sheep, have you any wool?

Yes sir, yes sir, ⌷4⌷ bags full.

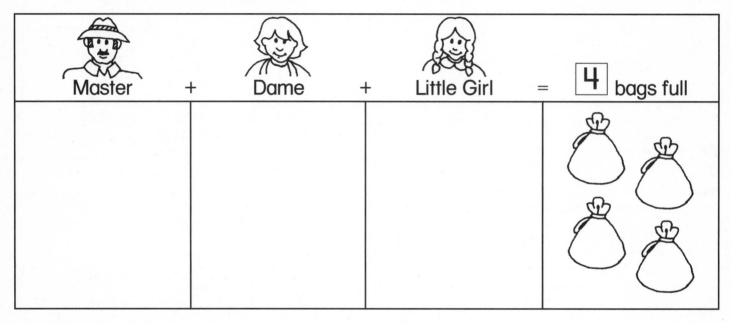

Master	+	Dame	+	Little Girl	=	⌷4⌷ bags full

2. Baa, baa, Black Sheep, have you any wool?

Yes sir, yes sir, ⌷6⌷ bags full.

Master	+	Dame	+	Little Girl	=	⌷6⌷ bags full

22

HICKORY DICKORY MATH   SCHOLASTIC PROFESSIONAL BOOKS

Counting Bags of Wool

3. Baa, baa, Black Sheep, have you any wool?

Yes sir, yes sir, [ ] bags full.

Master + Dame + Little Girl = [ ] bags full

Hickory Dickory Dock

Hickory Dickory Dock,
The mouse ran up the clock.
The clock struck one,
The mouse ran down.
Hickory Dickory Dock.

Hickory Dickory Dock,
The mouse ran up the clock.
The clock struck two,
The mouse cried "Boo Hoo!"
Hickory Dickory Dock.

Hickory Dickory Dock,
The mouse ran up the clock.
The clock struck three,
The mouse cried "Whee!"
Hickory Dickory Dock.

Hickory Dickory Dock,
The mouse ran up the clock.
The clock struck four,
The mouse fell to the floor.
Hickory Dickory Dock.

Hickory Dickory Dock,
The mouse ran up the clock.
The clock struck five,
The mouse took a dive.
Hickory Dickory Dock.

HICKORY DICKORY MATH   SCHOLASTIC PROFESSIONAL BOOKS

Hickory Dickory Dock

ENJOYING THE NURSERY RHYME

Distribute a copy of the rhyme to each child and invite children to "read" along as you read the poem. Ask children to find the number words *one, two, three, four, five.*

ACTIVITY   Telling Time

Children tell time to the hour.

Grouping: individual

Materials: Hickory Dickory Dock reproducible page 26, paper fasteners, scissors, thin cardboard, glue

Here's How:

1. Distribute copies of reproducible page 26, one paper fastener, scissors, cardboard, and glue to each child. Invite children to make their own Hickory Dickory Dock clocks.

2. Have children glue the reproducible to cardboard. When the glue dries, have them cut out the clock hands. Review that the longer hand is the minute hand and the shorter hand is the hour hand. Show children how to poke a small hole in the circle at the blunt end of each clock hand and in the circle at the center of the clockface. Help them position the hands over the center circle and secure with the paper fastener. Now children are ready to position the hands of their clocks to correspond with the verses as you reread the poem aloud.

Here's More:

* Ask children: What might the mouse be doing in the hour between his trips up the clock? As a class, make a list of things a mouse might do. For example, eating, sleeping, running from a cat, hiding from people, searching for cheese, and so on.

* Children might have fun estimating how long it would take a mouse to climb a refrigerator or run the distance of a room. To estimate this, students could pretend to be a mouse and act out the different activities.

* To help children understand duration of time, challenge them to figure out how many things a mouse could accomplish in one hour.

Assessment Ideas

* As you read the verses, walk around the room to check children's ability to position the hands of their clocks correctly to show the hours.
* Children can work with partners to check each other's work.

Math and Writing

As a journal entry, have children draw or write their own verses to show other activities of the mouse, complete with an illustration that depicts the time on a clockface. Children can share their work with the class.

Literature Links

A classic story that deals with time telling is Eric Carle's *The Grouchy Ladybug* (HarperCollins, 1977). Pat Hutchins's *Clocks and More Clocks* (Macmillan, 1970) tells the humorous story of a man who fills his house with clocks. And if children want to find out more about the clock-climbing mouse, Jim Aylesworth's *The Completed Hickory Dickory Dock* (Atheneum, 1990) will fill the bill.

Name _____

Hickory
Dickory
Dock

12   1   2   3   4   5   6   7   8   9   10   11

26

HICKORY DICKORY MATH   SCHOLASTIC PROFESSIONAL BOOKS

Humpty Dumpty

Humpty Dumpty sat on a wall,
Humpty Dumpty had a great fall.

All the king's horses
And all the king's men,
Couldn't put Humpty together again.

Humpty Dumpty

ENJOYING THE NURSERY RHYME

Read the poem aloud to your class. Ask children to suggest ways the king's men could put Humpty Dumpty together again. Explain to children that they will be doing an activity that will show one way to put Humpty Dumpty together. Distribute the poem, read it again, and invite children to read along.

ACTIVITY 1 Humpty Dumpty Tangrams

Children use geometry and logic to complete a tangram.

Grouping: individual

Materials: Humpty Dumpty Puzzle and Humpty Dumpty Tangram reproducible pages 29–30, glue, construction paper or tagboard squares cut to the same size as the tangram, scissors

Here's How:

1 Reread the Humpty Dumpty poem. Tell children that they'll use a picture puzzle to help figure out how to put Humpty Dumpty together.

2 Copy and distribute the tangram template and the picture puzzle of Humpty Dumpty from reproducible pages 29–30. Also distribute a square piece of construction paper or tagboard, scissors, and glue to each child. Have children cut out the tangram and the puzzle. Ask them to glue the tangram template onto one side of the piece of tagboard, and the Humpty Dumpty puzzle to the other side. Make sure the glue covers the entire surface so that the individual pieces won't come off after the tangram is cut apart.

3 When the glue dries, tell children to cut along the dotted lines of the tangram template to make the separate tangram pieces.

4 Ask children to mix up the pieces of the tangram and then put them together again. Children can start by using the Humpty Dumpty puzzle as their guide. As they become more proficient, they can make a square by putting the tangram shapes together correctly.

Assessment Ideas

Ask children to identify the shapes that make up the tangram. Can they find similar shapes around the room?

MATH ACTIVITY CENTER Tangram Workshop

Make another tangram using a solid color of construction paper. Trace and cut apart the tangram pieces and then place the pieces in an envelope. Also have available pencils, sheets of paper, and pictures similar to the ones below made from tangram shapes.

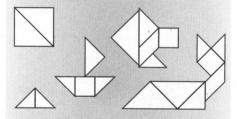

Invite children to use the tangram that you've provided to make either the classic tangram shapes you've modeled for them or shapes all their own! As children invent shapes, they can trace or copy them onto the paper. Display the class creations in the hallway for all to see.

Literature Link

Children will be inspired to use their tangram pieces to make realistic and imaginary animals of their own after hearing Ann Tombert's *Grandfather Tang's Story* (Crown, 1990). This tale recounts the story of two animals who change their shapes as they chase each other.

Name _____

Humpty Dumpty Puzzle

HICKORY DICKORY MATH   SCHOLASTIC PROFESSIONAL BOOKS

Humpty Dumpty Tangram

HICKORY DICKORY MATH   SCHOLASTIC PROFESSIONAL BOOKS

ACTIVITY 2 Humpty Dumpty Fractions

Children identify halves, fourths, and eighths.

Grouping: individual

Materials: Humpty Dumpty Fractions reproducible page 32, scissors

Here's How:

1 Distribute reproducible page 32 to each child. Review the fractions that are represented by each picture. In the first picture, Humpty Dumpty is shown as one complete circle, or one whole. In the second picture, Humpty is cut into two equal pieces: each piece is one half of the whole. The third picture shows four equal pieces: each piece is one fourth of the whole. The last picture shows eight equal pieces: each piece is one eighth of the whole.

2 Ask children to cut apart the fraction pieces for halves, fourths, and eighths. Remind them to keep the first picture intact to use as a model or guide.

3 Invite children to put the fraction pieces together by finding combinations of fractions that will give them a complete (whole) circle again. For example, children might put together one half and two fourths to make one whole Humpty Dumpty.

4 After children have had time to try various combinations, ask them to share their findings. Draw diagrams on the chalkboard to represent the combinations of halves, fourths, and eighths that make one whole.

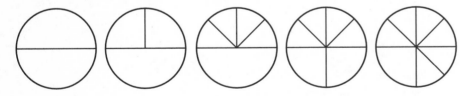

Here's More:

Build awareness of equivalent fractions by challenging children to find the following:

☀ How many quarters make one half?

☀ How many eighths make one half?

☀ How many eighths make one quarter?

Assessment Ideas

How many combinations were children able to find to complete one whole? Ask them to review how many halves, quarters, and eighths make one whole.

MATH ACTIVITY CENTER

Cracker Fractions

Using construction paper, cut out round, square, and rectangular patterns to represent one half, four quarters, and eight eighths. For each pattern, provide a complete whole "cracker" marked with the fractions and cut-apart fraction pieces. Put each whole and its fractions in separate envelopes. Explain to children that they should use the pieces to find different ways to make one whole.

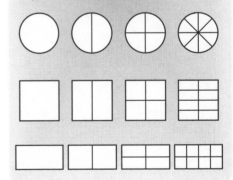

Literature Links

A wonderful book full of more puzzles, including another Humpty Dumpty puzzle, is *The Rebus Treasury* by Jean Marzollo (Dial, 1986). Good books to reinforce fraction concepts are *Eating Fractions* by Bruce McMillan (Scholastic, 1991) and *Fraction Action* by Loreen Leedy (Holiday House, 1994).

Humpty Dumpty Fractions

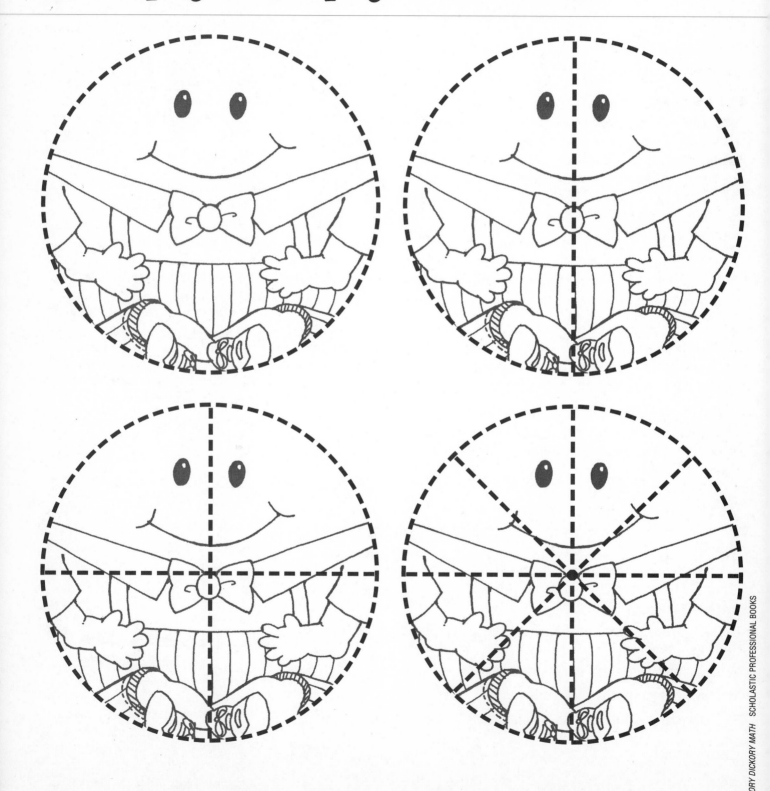

The Ugly Duckling

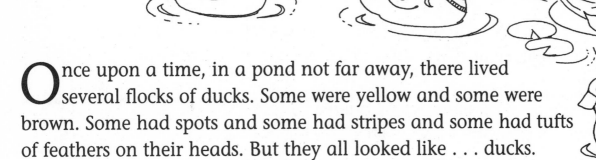

Once upon a time, in a pond not far away, there lived several flocks of ducks. Some were yellow and some were brown. Some had spots and some had stripes and some had tufts of feathers on their heads. But they all looked like . . . ducks.

One day, a mother duck sitting on her nest of eggs noticed something unusual: an egg that was much, much larger than any of her others. Although she wondered where the enormous egg had come from, she protected it as if it was one of her own.

Time passed, and the mother duck's eggs began to hatch. Nine little yellow ducklings popped out of their eggs. They peeped and cheeped happily. But there was one more egg to hatch. Can you guess which one it was? The mother duck waited, and waited, and waited some more. Just as she was about to give up, she heard a crack.

Now, all the other ducks on the pond were quite curious. They had greeted the nine new baby ducklings, and they wanted to say hello to the tenth. As they crowded closer, a huge head popped out from the last egg! All of the ducks gasped in fright. The tenth baby was the ugliest duckling they had ever seen! The ducks swam away to the other side of the pond.

Mother duck took a good look at her new baby. He did indeed look different from her other ducklings. He was bigger, and he

had big feet and a long neck. But he was as sweet as her other babies, and she loved him even though he was unusual.

But the other ducks called the newcomer the Ugly Duckling because he was big and clumsy. They made fun of his long neck and his big feet. They played with the nine yellow ducklings, but they laughed at the Ugly Duckling's dull gray feathers.

One day, some of the other ducks surrounded the Ugly Duckling. "What kind of duck are you?" they asked. "You don't have tufts on your head like some of us. You don't have spots like some of us. You don't have stripes like some of us. You aren't like any of us, so why don't you leave!"

Sadly, the Ugly Duckling did. He wandered for a very long time, until he reached another pond. There he lived all alone, through the spring, then summer, then fall, and even through the long, hard winter.

As spring began again, the Ugly Duckling found himself surrounded by the most beautiful birds he had ever seen! They were huge. Their necks were long and graceful. They had large webbed feet. And their feathers gleamed a bright, beautiful white.

The Ugly Duckling felt ashamed again. He tried to hide himself in the weeds, so the others would not see how ugly he was.

The beautiful birds swam toward him. As he tried to hide, he looked down and saw his own reflection in the pond. The Ugly Duckling could not believe his eyes. He was not an Ugly Duckling anymore. In fact, he was not a duck at all! He was a swan! And indeed, he was the most handsome swan on the pond.

The Ugly Duckling

ENJOYING THE FAIRY TALE

Read the story of the Ugly Duckling to your class. Talk with children about why the ducks thought the new baby was ugly. Stress that the baby was not really ugly, but rather just different looking. Remind them that the baby became a beautiful swan. You may want to copy the story for children to take home and reread with a family member.

ACTIVITY 1 Finding the Ugly Duckling

Children sort and classify by attributes.

Grouping: pairs

Materials: The Ugly Duckling reproducible page 36, crayons, scissors

Here's How:

1 Ask children to recall some of the characteristics of the adult ducks from the story. If necessary, reread the paragraphs that describe them. Talk with children about the characteristics of the Ugly Duckling that made him different. Tell children they'll look at some pictures of ducks and find the Ugly Duckling. To do this, they'll put the other ducks into groups. The one that doesn't fit into any of the groups is the Ugly Duckling.

2 Divide the class into pairs. Distribute a copy of reproducible page 36 and scissors to each pair. Talk with children about the characteristics of some of the ducks they see. Then ask children to cut apart the small squares so they have a flock of ducks. Ask them to suggest ways to put all the ducks into groups so that the ducks within a group are alike in some way. For example, children might suggest a group of ducks that have striped necks or a group of ducks with spots.

3 Give children time to make their groups. Then invite volunteers to explain the groups they made. Also ask children to find the bird that has not been put in a group. That one is the Ugly Duckling!

4 Children can color all the ducks in each group a particular color to add another characteristic that will make the ducks within a group alike. Collect and save the ducks for Activity 2.

Assessment Ideas

Were children able to group all of the ducks except one? What characteristics did children use as they made their groups? Were they able to explain how the ducks in each group are alike?

Math and Writing

Explain that people often use an animal's physical traits to name species of animals. You may want to use a field guide to birds to show some birds whose popular names reveal their traits: robin redbreast, bluebird, blue jay, spoonbill, horned owl, blackbird.

Ask children to invent names for the different duck groups they cut out from the activity sheet. The names can be highly imaginative or straightforward. Ask children to explain why they think a particular name is a good one.

Literature Links

A classroom button collection makes a wonderful sorting activity. And you can read Margarette Reid's *The Button Box* (Dutton, 1990) to share how one boy sorts the buttons in his grandmother's button box. *Just a Mess* by Mercer Mayer (Western, 1987) will demonstrate for children how important it is to have a logical classification plan.

The Ugly Duckling

ACTIVITY 2 Graphing Ducks

Children graph, count, add, and subtract.

Grouping: pairs

Materials: cut-apart ducks from Activity 1, large sheets of
construction paper, glue

Here's How:

1. Redistribute children's cut-apart ducks from the previous
activity. Also give them a sheet of construction paper and glue.
Ask them to make rows of ducks, going from left to right, on the
paper. Each row should contain ducks that are the same. Have children place their ducks in rows, then check their work before they glue
the ducks onto the construction paper.

2. Ask volunteers to explain what the pictograph shows. After
children have shared their ideas, ask them to use their graphs
to answer questions like these:

- Which kind of duck is there the most of? Which kind is there the
fewest of?

- How many ducks have spots? How many have tufts on their heads?
How many more ducks have spots than tufts?

- If we put together a group of ringed ducks and a group of spotted
ducks, how many ducks would there be in all?

Here's More:

Work with the class to make number sentences for the subtraction and
addition situations in your questions. For example:

Assessment Ideas

Answers to the questions in
step 2 should give an indication of how
familiar children are with the concepts
of *more* and *fewer*. Notice what tech-
niques children are using to answer
questions that involve subtraction and
addition.

Literature Link

Eric Carle's *Rooster's Off to
See the World* (Picture Book Studio,
1972) recounts the tale of a rooster
who is joined by animal friends—first
one, then two, then three, and so on—
as he goes off to see the world. Bright
visuals are accompanied by black-and-
white pictographs that record the number of each kind of animal.

$$5 + 4 = 9$$

ACTIVITY 3 Duck Venn Diagrams

Children sort and classify using Venn diagrams.

Grouping: 5 groups

Materials: Duck Template reproducible page 39, crayons or paint, scissors, glue, two 4-foot lengths of yarn or string

Here's How:

1 Give each child a copy of reproducible page 39. Tell the class that they will cut out, assemble, and color their ducks according to your directions. Then divide the class into 5 groups and assign each group characteristics to add to their ducks. Use these characteristics:

❀ **Group 1**—yellow ducks with smooth wings

❀ **Group 2**—white ducks with ruffled wings and ringed necks

❀ **Group 3**—white ducks with smooth wings and spots

❀ **Group 4**—yellow ducks with ruffled wings

❀ **Group 5**—brown ducks with smooth wings and ringed necks

Note: It is important that children color the ducks as directed so the characteristics will form intersecting groups for the Venn diagram. Children can have a second template to decorate as they like.

2 When children have finished their ducks, make two overlapping yarn or string circles on the floor. Gather children in a circle so everyone can see the Venn diagram you are creating. Place a yellow duck on one side of the Venn diagram. Ask children to describe it. Then place a white duck with spots on the other side of the Venn diagram. Again ask children to talk about that duck's characteristics.

3 Now hold up a duck that is yellow with spots. Talk with children about where the third duck should go—in the first circle, with yellow ducks, or in the second circle, with ducks having spots? Help children to see that the duck can be placed in the overlapping part of the circles, because it shares characteristics of both other ducks.

4 Repeat the activity with other ducks children have made. Each time, ask children to explain "rules" for grouping. What characteristics does a duck have to be placed in the first circle? To be placed in the second circle? When will a duck go in the center, overlapping portion of the Venn diagram? What happens if a duck has none of the characteristics of either group?

Math and Art

You might give each child another copy of the Duck Template and materials such as wiggly eyes, craft feathers, and construction paper scraps to create their own individual ducks to take home or decorate the classroom.

Literature Link

Jean Marzollo's *I Spy School Days: A Book of Picture Riddles* (Scholastic, 1995) has a great example of a Venn diagram in a wonderful rhyming game format.

yellow duck   yellow duck with spots   white duck with spots

Name _____

Duck Template

Goldilocks and the Three Bears

Once upon a time, there were three bears: Papa Bear, Mama Bear, and wee little Baby Bear. The three bears lived in a charming house in the woods.

One day, after making their breakfast porridge, the bears went for a walk. While they were out, a little girl named Goldilocks came to their house.

Goldilocks knocked on the door, and when no one answered, she went inside. She had been walking for a long time and was very tired. In the living room, she found three chairs. One chair was very large. She tried to climb up into it, but it was too tall. The middle-sized chair was easier for her to get into but hard for her to climb out of. Finally, Goldilocks saw a wee little chair. That chair was just the right size. She rested there for a while.

Then Goldilocks realized that she was very hungry. She jumped up out of the wee little chair and knocked it over, breaking it all to pieces.

In the bears' kitchen, there were three bowls of porridge. The first bowl was so big Goldilocks could barely see over the top. And the porridge in it was much too hot to eat. So she went on to the next bowl, a middle-sized bowl. But the porridge in that bowl was cold, much too cold to eat. And so she went on to the last bowl. It was a wee little bowl, and the porridge was just the right temperature! Goldilocks gobbled it all up.

When Goldilocks finished eating, she felt sleepy. In the bears' bedroom, the first bed she came to was huge! Goldilocks climbed up

into it, but the bed was much too hard. Goldilocks went on to the next bed. The middle-sized bed was easier to get into, but it was much too soft. Finally, Goldilocks spotted a wee little bed that looked just right. And it was! She climbed into it, lay down, and fell fast asleep.

As Goldilocks slept, the three bears came home. The first thing they noticed was their chairs. "Someone has been sitting in my chair!" roared Papa Bear. Mama Bear complained, "Someone has been sitting in my chair, too!" And Baby bear cried, "Wah! Someone has been sitting in my chair and broken it into wee little pieces!"

Next the bears went into the kitchen. Papa Bear roared, "Someone has tasted my bowl of porridge!" Mama Bear complained, "Someone has tasted my bowl of porridge, too!" And Baby Bear cried, "Someone has tasted my bowl of porridge and has eaten it all up!"

The Three Bears went upstairs to their bedroom, not knowing what they would find. Papa Bear roared, "Someone has been sleeping in my bed!" Mama Bear complained, "Someone has been sleeping in my bed, too!" And Baby Bear cried, "Someone has been sleeping in my bed, and she's still there!"

Well, not for long! The bears' voices woke Goldilocks. She jumped out of the bed and ran straight home.

Goldilocks and the Three Bears

ENJOYING THE FAIRY TALE

Read the story of Goldilocks and the Three Bears to your class. Ask which bear children think was most upset at the end of the story, and why. Then talk with children about the comparative sizes of the bears and their belongings. If Papa Bear is the biggest bear, Mama Bear is the middle-sized bear, and Baby Bear is the smallest, ask children how they would decide who owned each chair, porridge bowl, and bed. After they share their ideas, give each child a copy of the story to take home and read with family members.

As a fun follow-up to the story, invite children to bring in their own stuffed bears. Use them for counting and graphing activities.

ACTIVITY 1 How the Bears Measure Up

Children compare sizes of bears, chairs, and bowls.

Grouping: individual

Materials: 3 chairs, 3 bowls, drawing paper, crayons

Here's How:

1 Gather three chairs of varying sizes and three bowls of varying sizes. Place them where all children can see them. Reread the story of Goldilocks and the Three Bears. As you read the parts of the story about the bears' chairs and bowls, pause. Draw attention to the three chairs and three bowls you have displayed. Ask children which they think is Papa Bear's chair and bowl, Mama Bear's chair and bowl, and Baby Bear's chair and bowl.

2 Ask children to think of household items that the three bears each might own: for example, spoons, toothbrushes, cups. Distribute drawing paper and crayons and invite children to make their own drawings of one particular item for each of the three bears. Based on each object's size, ask them to label their items *Papa Bear*, *Mama Bear*, and *Baby Bear*.

3 When children's drawings are complete, ask volunteers to show their pictures and to tell why they think each item is suitable for a particular bear.

MATH ACTIVITY CENTER More Measuring

In the math center, provide 12-inch rulers and yardsticks. Make a reproducible recording sheet with rebus pictures of common classroom objects: desk, table, chair, book, scissors, crayon, and so on. Provide copies of the reproducible in the center. Encourage children to take a recording sheet and use the ruler or yardstick to measure the actual objects and record the number of inches tall or long each object measures.

Literature Links

Good books for discussions of comparative size include Tana Hoban's *Is It Larger? Is It Smaller?* (Greenwillow, 1985) and Leo Lionni's *The Biggest House in the World* (Pantheon, 1968). Relative size is highlighted in *Spence Is Small* by Christa Chevalier (Albert Whitman, 1987).

ACTIVITY 2 Comparing Bowls of Porridge

Children estimate and compare volume.

Grouping: whole class

Materials: pint, quart, and gallon containers; foam packing pellets (or substitute uniform-shaped cereal such as Cheerios or Kix)

Here's How:

1 On the chalkboard, write *First Guess*, *Second Guess*, *Final Answer*. Display the three containers and ask children to imagine that these are Papa Bear's, Mama Bear's, and Baby Bear's bowls.

2 You may want to use the terms *pint*, *quart*, and *gallon*. Or you may refer to the containers informally as bowls for the bears. Fill the pint container with packing pellets or cereal. Ask the class how many pints (Baby Bear bowls) it will take to fill the quart (Mama Bear's bowl). Have children guess. Write their guesses on the chalkboard under *First Guess*.

3 Pour the contents of Baby Bear's bowl into Mama Bear's bowl. Ask the class how many pints they think will fit into Mama Bear's bowl now. Write their guesses under *Second Guess*. If children's estimates are different the first and second time, discuss the differences.

4 Now actually fill Mama Bear's bowl using Baby Bear's bowl to measure quantity. Ask children to count how many Baby Bear bowls it took to fill Mama Bear's bowl. Write the correct amount on the board under *Final Answer*.

5 Repeat the activity using Mama Bear bowls and Papa Bear bowls. Record children's guesses and then do the actual measuring again.

6 Finally, ask children to estimate how many Baby Bear bowls they think it will take to fill Papa Bear's bowl. Ask volunteers to explain their reasoning. You may want to fill Papa Bear's bowl using Baby Bear's bowl. Ask any children who made a correct estimate to explain how they figured out the answer.

Here's More:

Using items such as popcorn kernels, sand, or water, illustrate the relationship among pints, quarts, and gallons. Point out that it doesn't matter what is put into the units of measure. Each time, the number of pints it takes to fill a quart or a gallon is the same.

Measuring Volume

Leave the measuring containers and cereal or packing pellets in the math center. Provide additional containers. Allow children to work in pairs to measure amounts each container holds and record their findings.

Literature Link

For an interesting perspective on the concept of volume, read Steven Kellogg's *The Mysterious Tadpole* (Dial, 1977), in which the title character outgrows a series of containers.

ACTIVITY 3 Tasty Temperatures

Children estimate and compare temperature.

Grouping: individual

Materials: Tasty Temperatures reproducible pages 45–46, pencils, scissors, glue, thermometer (optional)

Here's How:

1 Ask children to recall the part of the story of Goldilocks and the Three Bears when Goldilocks tasted the bears' porridge. What did she notice about the temperature of each bowl of porridge? Display a thermometer or a picture of a thermometer and remind children that it is a tool used to measure temperature. Point out where the red line of the thermometer might be if the temperature is low (cold), relative to where it might be if the temperature is warmer (just right) or high (hot).

Literature Link
Nicki Weiss's *On a Hot, Hot Day* (Putnam, 1992) will inspire a discussion of fun things to do on very hot and very cold days.

2 Distribute reproducible pages 45 and 46. Ask children to imagine that Papa Bear always likes things that are too hot, Mama Bear likes things that are too cold, and Baby Bear likes things that are just right. With these clues in mind, as a class, go over the first activity page and ask children to tell what temperature each bear's thermometer shows (high or hot for Papa Bear, and so on). Have children look at the second activity page and decide which food items could belong to each bear. Ask them to cut out the pictures and glue them under the appropriate bear.

Here's More:

You might want to use an actual thermometer to point out that in a Fahrenheit scale, the scale most widely used in the United States, 32°F is the temperature where water freezes, and 212°F is where water boils. Use these, and the temperature in your classroom, as a frame of reference for "too hot," "too cold," and "just right" temperatures.

Tasty Temperatures

Papa Bear	Mama Bear	Baby Bear

Tasty Temperatures

HICKORY DICKORY MATH   SCHOLASTIC PROFESSIONAL BOOKS

The Three Little Pigs

Once upon a time, there were three little pigs. When they were all grown up, their mother sent them off into the world to make homes of their own.

The First Little Pig met a man with a bundle of straw. "Please sir, may I have some straw to build a house?" asked the First Little Pig. And so the First Little Pig built his house of straw.

The Second Little Pig met a man with a bundle of sticks. "Please sir, can I have some sticks to build a house?" asked the Second Little Pig. And so the Second Little Pig built his house of sticks.

Now the Third Little Pig thought carefully about what he should use to build a sturdy house. He found a man with a load of bricks. "Please sir, would you sell these bricks to me to build a house?" And so the Third Little Pig built his house of bricks.

Since the First Little Pig built his house of straw, it didn't take him long to finish the job. He was napping the day away when he heard a knock on the door.

"Little pig, little pig, let me in," said a Big Bad Wolf.

The First Little Pig was frightened. "I'll huff, and I'll puff, and I'll blow your house in," the wolf called. The First Little Pig managed to leap from his bed just as the Big Bad Wolf blew his house in.

Then the First Little Pig ran and ran, until he reached the home

HICKORY DICKORY MATH SCHOLASTIC PROFESSIONAL BOOKS

of the Second Little Pig. They had just enough time to lock the Second Little Pig's front door when the Big Bad Wolf arrived.

"Little pigs, little pigs, let me in," said the wolf.

The two Little Pigs were frightened. "I'll huff and I'll puff and I'll blow your house in," called the wolf. The Second Little Pig grabbed the hand of the First Little Pig, and out the back door they went!

Then the two pigs ran and ran, until they reached the house of the Third Little Pig. They went into the sturdy brick house and locked the front door.

A few moments later, the Big Bad Wolf arrived and knocked on the door.

"Little pigs, little pigs, let me in!" the wolf roared. When the pigs refused, the wolf roared, "I'll huff and I'll puff and I'll blow your house in!"

Well, the wolf huffed and he puffed, and he puffed and he

huffed. But there was no way he could blow the brick house in! Out of breath, the wolf finally gave up and decided he would find an easier meal somewhere else. And the three little pigs lived together happily ever after, in the sturdy brick house.

48

The Three Little Pigs

ENJOYING THE FAIRY TALE

Read the story of the Three Little Pigs to your class. Encourage children to talk about the building materials each pig used. Discuss why the brick house was sturdier than the houses built of straw or sticks. Give each child a copy of the story to take home and enjoy.

ACTIVITY 1 A House that's Wolfproof

Children use geometry to find a sturdy shape.

Grouping: pairs

Materials: miniature marshmallows, toothpicks (Stale marshmallows work best. Spread marshmallows on paper or a tray to dry out overnight. Or substitute balls of clay for the marshmallows.)

Here's How:

1 Ahead of time, make a toothpick triangle and square.

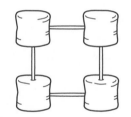 

2 Recall with the class the reason the wolf was able to blow down the house of straw and the house of sticks. Explain to children that just as some building materials make stronger houses than others, some shapes are "stronger" than others. Hold up the toothpick triangle and rectangle and ask children to guess which is stronger. Ask the reasons for their answers.

3 Divide the class in pairs. Assign one child in each pair to make the triangle and the other one to make the square. Distribute materials and model how to make each shape if necessary.

4 When shapes are completed, show children how to push gently on the top of each shape. What happens? As children see that the square collapses more easily, what conclusions can they draw about which shape is stronger?

Math and Social Studies

Show children pictures of structures that have been built using triangular shapes: for example, the pyramids, bridges that have triangular supports, girders that form building supports, and so on.

To make a real-life connection, you might ask an engineer, contractor, architect, or other building professional to talk with your class about the importance of geometry. Ask the speaker to emphasize concepts, such as the strength of different materials and shapes, in language that is age-appropriate for the children.

Literature Links

Shapes are included in buildings for both practical reasons and reasons of design and proportion. Read to your class Philip Isaacson's *Round Buildings, Square Buildings, and Buildings That Wiggle Like a Fish* (Knopf, 1988). What are some familiar and not-so-familiar shapes, and what do they resemble? To find out, read Bodel Rikys's *Red Bear's Fun With Shapes* (Dial, 1993).

ACTIVITY 2 The Little Pigs' House Takes Shape

Children use geometry and estimation skills to estimate area.

Grouping: individual

Materials: The Little Pigs' House Takes Shape reproducible page 51; pencils; scissors; construction paper cutouts of a circle, triangle, and square

Here's How:

1 Recall with children that in the story of the Three Little Pigs, all three pigs gathered in the strong brick house of the Third Little Pig. Ask children what might have happened if his house had not been big enough for all of them.

2 Show children the cutouts of a circle, triangle, and square and ask volunteers to name them. Then ask which one they think covers the most space. Explain that one way to decide how big a house is would be to measure how big the floor is. If the pigs' homes could have a floor in the shape of a square, a circle, or a triangle, ask children which shape they think would cover the most space. Take a vote and record children's choices. If they have math journals, have children record their guesses in their journals.

3 Distribute reproducible page 51. Ask children to count the number of complete squares within each of the three shapes. If there are pieces of a shape that are not complete squares, tell children to match pieces with other pieces to try to make additional whole squares for counting. Some children may find it easier to count if they first cut out the three shapes.

4 Have children fill in the chart by recording the number of squares in each shape. Ask children to compare their findings with their original estimates. Which shape did they think would cover the most area? Which shape actually did?

Assessment Ideas

To see if children understand the concept of area as it applies to the three shapes, ask them which floor they would have to buy the most carpeting for if they wanted to cover the whole floor. If children have difficulty counting squares, encourage them to count only complete squares. They can use inch-square counting tiles to cover as many of the squares as possible within the circle, square, and triangle on the reproducible.

Math and Writing

Invite children to draw or write their own version of the Three Little Pigs story to include their mathematical findings, or as a class, write a story together. A new story might include more than three little pigs, or it might be a story about houses of different shapes rather than different building materials.

Literature Links

What happens when *four* little pigs set out to build their houses? A wonderful spin-off of the Three Little Pigs tale is *The Fourth Little Pig* written by Teresa Celsi (Raintree/Steck-Vaughn, 1992). In this version, the three little pigs hide in the Third Little Pig's house and are rescued by their sister, the Fourth Little Pig.

The Little Pigs' House Takes Shape

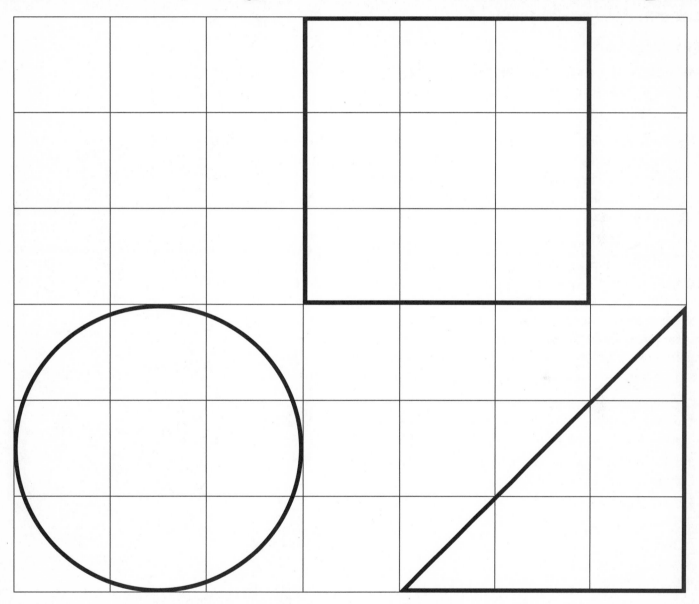

Shape	⬤	◼	◣
Number of Squares in Each			

ACTIVITY 3 Housing Combos

Children make combinations.

Grouping: pairs

Materials: Housing Combos reproducible page 53, scissors, paper and pencils, three shirts and three pants brought from home

Here's How:

1 Display the clothing you have brought and ask the class how many different outfits they think could be made from combinations of three shirts and three pants. Record children's guesses. Then actually place different shirts and pants together to show the 9 outfits that can be made.

2 Divide the class into pairs and give each pair a copy of the reproducible, scissors, a piece of paper, and a pencil. Help children identify the three types of houses (straw, sticks, bricks) and the three types of roofs (thatch, shingle, tile) on the page. Ask children to imagine that these are choices of housing and roofs for the three little pigs. If the pigs picked the same type of roof for each of their houses, how many combinations could they make? Ask children to cut out the houses and roofs and try it. Now ask children to consider these questions:

❋ What if the pigs had two choices of roofs for each of their houses? How many combinations could they make?

❋ What if the pigs had three choices of roofs? How many combinations could they make?

Have children use their cutouts to model each situation.

3 Have children record on paper or in their journals what they discovered about making combinations.

Here's More:

Add another element and ask children to experiment with more combinations. For example, what if the pigs have a choice of a round or square window for each house? With three types of house, three types of roof, and two types of window, how many different combinations can be made? This would be a good activity to demonstrate for the whole class. Have a record keeper keep track of the combinations. Children will see that without a list or chart it becomes difficult to avoid repeating combinations.

Clothing Combos

Provide other materials for children to experiment with combinations. Commercial or homemade paper dolls provide a good way for children to test different outfits that can be made. Old clothing from the dress-up corner can also be used. Set out small sets of shirts, pants, and hats, for example, and encourage children to make lists or charts to keep track of the clothing combinations they make.

Literature Link

To further illustrate the idea of different types of homes, look for *This Is My House* by Arthur Dorros (Scholastic, 1992). It teaches children how to say the book's title in 13 different languages, while showing them 13 different homes around the world.

Name _____

Housing Combos

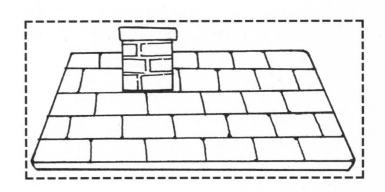

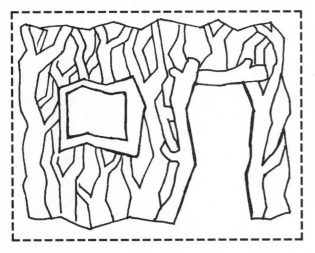

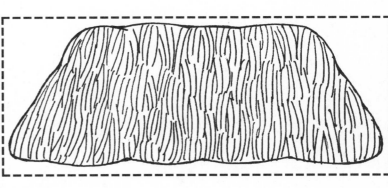

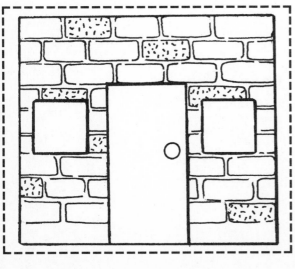

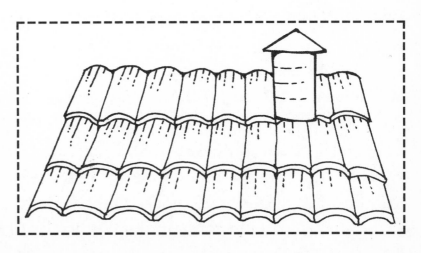

HICKORY DICKORY MATH   SCHOLASTIC PROFESSIONAL BOOKS

53

Little Red Riding Hood

Once upon a time, there lived a little girl. She was called Little Red Riding Hood, because she wore a red coat with a hood, made for her by her dear grandmother.

One day Little Red's mother gave her a basket of food to bring to her grandmother's house. As she set off, Red's mother warned her not to stop to pick flowers or apples. She told Little Red to go straight to her grandmother's house, and Little Red promised that she would.

As Little Red went on her way, a voice called to her. "Hello there, little girl! Where are you going with that basket of goodies?" And who was talking, but a big, hungry wolf!

Red told the wolf, "I'm going to my grandma's house. She lives on the other side of the woods. And I must be going, since I promised I would go straight to Grandma's house."

At that, the wolf bounded off. Little Red continued on her way. She didn't know that as she walked, the wolf arrived at her grandmother's house. He knocked on the door, and when Grandma told him to come in, he pounced! Luckily, Grandma got out of the house and ran away from the wolf.

HICKORY DICKORY MATH   SCHOLASTIC PROFESSIONAL BOOKS

The wolf, still very hungry, decided to pounce on Little Red instead. He dressed up in Grandma's clothes and eyeglasses and waited in Grandma's bed for Little Red.

When Little Red knocked on the door, the wolf called to her. "Who is it?" asked the wolf, in his best grandma voice.

"Grandma, it is me, Little Red Riding Hood. I have come with goodies for you," called Little Red. She opened the front door and walked to her grandmother's bedroom. She stood by her grandmother's bed.

"Why Grandma, what big ears you have!" said Little Red.

"The better to hear you with, my dear," said the wolf.

"Why Grandma, what big eyes you have!" said Little Red.

"The better to see you with, my dear," replied the wolf.

"Why Grandma, what big teeth you have!" shrieked Red.

"The better to eat you with!" growled the wolf, as he sprang from the bed toward Little Red.

Just then a man, whom Grandma met in the woods, arrived at Grandma's house. He captured the wolf and carried him off, far away. And the wolf never bothered Little Red Riding Hood and her grandmother again.

Little Red Riding Hood

ENJOYING THE FAIRY TALE

Read the story of Little Red Riding Hood to your class. In this version of the classic tale, Little Red's mother cautions her to go straight to Grandma's house. You might set up two chairs at opposite ends of the room. Ask a volunteer to walk straight from one chair to the other. Ask another volunteer to take a different path. Talk with children about why they think it was important for Little Red Riding Hood to go straight to her grandmother's house.

ACTIVITY Reading Little Red's Map

Children use map reading, measurement, and addition skills.

Grouping: individual

Materials: Little Red Riding Hood's Map reproducible page 57, four different colors of crayons, rulers

Here's How:

1. After reading the tale of Little Red Riding Hood, distribute reproducible page 57. Ask children to look at the map and identify Little Red Riding Hood's house and Grandma's house. Ask them also to identify other landmarks they can find on the map: the lily pond, the patch of wildflowers, the apple tree.

2. Explain that the map shows several paths Little Red could take to Grandma's house. Ask children which path they think is the shortest. Then invite them to check their guess by finding the length of each path.

3. Ask volunteers to identify the lengths of various paths. As a path is discussed, have children use a crayon to trace it. For example:
- How long is the path that passes the pond? Trace that path with a red crayon.
- Which is the shortest path? How long is it? Trace that path with a blue crayon.

Here's More:

You can have children use inch rulers to determine the actual measurements of each path. For all but the path that goes straight between the two houses, they will have to measure and add to find the total number of inches.

Assessment Ideas

Were children able to find the paths as you and their classmates identified them? Did children use counting or addition strategies to find the length of each path? Could children identify the shortest path? Could they explain why this was the shortest?

Math and Writing

On a separate piece of paper or in their math journals, tell children to write equations for the paths they found. For example: 4 + 3 + 1 + 4 = 12

Literature Links

An adorable book by Loreen Leedy called *The Bunny Play* (Holiday House, 1988) uses the story of Little Red Riding Hood to show what it takes to put on a play. *Lon Po Po* by Ed Young (Putnam, 1989) is a version of the Little Red Riding Hood story told in China.

Name _____

Little Red Riding Hood's Map

The Pied Piper of Hamelin

L ong ago, in a land far away, there was a village called Hamelin. For many years, Hamelin was a wonderful place to live. But one year, for reasons unknown to the citizens, rats settled in the town.

At first there were only one or two rats. But in just a few short weeks, the village had hundreds of them! Soon the townsfolk could not walk without rats scurrying from underfoot.

The citizens called a meeting in the town square. They complained to the mayor and demanded he take action. Just as the mayor was about to speak, a stranger stepped from the crowd.

The stranger wore a large-brimmed hat that covered most of his head and face. But from what the townsfolk could see of his face, the man had a long pointy face—much like that of a rat. He carried a flutelike pipe.

To the mayor and to all of the townspeople the stranger said, "I can rid your town of these rats."

The mayor said, "We have tried many ways to get rid of the rats and we have failed. What can you do that we have not already tried?"

HICKORY DICKORY MATH   SCHOLASTIC PROFESSIONAL BOOKS

The man replied, "I will use my pipe to lead them out of town. In return you must pay me whatever I wish for each rat that I take."

The townsfolk gasped in surprise. How much money might the piper ask for? But without hesitation, the mayor said, "We must rid our town of these rats. But before we agree to pay you, you must show us that this can be done."

The piper bowed to the mayor and began to play on his pipe. Twelve rats ran to the piper and stood before him. As he played, they formed lines, much like a marching band in a parade.

The mayor and townspeople watched in awe as the piper mysteriously seemed to be able to tell the rats what to do, just by playing on his pipe. After such a show, the mayor agreed to pay the piper whatever he wished.

And that night, all of the townspeople watched from their windows as the Pied Piper led a parade of hundreds of rats out of their town forever.

The Pied Piper of Hamelin

ENJOYING THE FAIRY TALE

Read the story of the Pied Piper to your class. Ask them to guess what the piper might have asked for in return for taking the rats from the town of Hamelin. Give each child a copy of the story to take home and enjoy with family members.

ACTIVITY 1 Combinations on Parade!

Children form a parade to find combinations to make 12.

Grouping: whole class

Here's How:

1 Remind children of the part of the story when the Pied Piper shows the citizens of Hamelin how he uses his pipe to make the rats do as he wishes. Twelve rats lined up in different combinations and marched for the piper.

2 Invite 12 children to come to the front of the class and line up in different ways to see how many ways they can make 12. For example:

❀ march in one straight line of 12

❀ march in three rows with the same number in each row

❀ march in two rows with the same number in each row

❀ march in three rows with each row having one more than the preceding row

As each marching formation is named, help children arrange themselves into rows. Ask the rest of the class to see if the rows are correct.

3 Have children keep a record of the different combinations they model. The activity can demonstrate addition sentences and can give a beginning look at multiplication: a given number of equal groups. Have children use counters if you want to model the combinations in step 2.

Here's More:

After the class has exhausted the combinations for 12, provide more practice using other numbers, for example, 8, 15, 16, 20.

Assessment Ideas

Were children able to form the combinations you asked for? Could they model combinations on their own? Ask children to demonstrate some of their combinations with counters.

Literature Links

A wonderful tale called *Two Hundred Rabbits* by Lonzo Anderson and Adrienne Adams (Viking, 1968) could be used to enhance the activity. In this story, a young man eager to please the king uses a magic whistle to bring 200 rabbits marching in rows to the royal court. And Elinor Pinczes's *One Hundred Hungry Ants* (Houghton Mifflin, 1993) shows how hungry ants figure out how to march more quickly by rearranging themselves.

ACTIVITY 2 Paying the Piper

Children count and add money.

Grouping: individual

Materials: Paying the Piper and Money for the Piper reproducible pages 62–63, pencils, paper, play money (optional)

Here's How:

1 Distribute a copy of reproducible page 62 to each child. Explain that these are groups of rats the Pied Piper led out of Hamelin. Tell children they'll help the mayor figure out how much money he'll have to pay the piper.

2 Ask volunteers to count the number of rats on the page, or count them together as a class. Ask children if they see any shortcuts for counting. If children have worked with base-ten blocks, they may see that they can count by tens more easily than by ones.

3 Now have children use play money, or cut out coins from reproducible page 63. With their coins, ask children to figure out how much money the town will have to pay in each of the following situations:

❋ How much would the people have to pay the piper if he asked for a penny for each group of 10 rats?

❋ How much would the people have to pay the piper if he asked for a nickel for each group of 10 rats?

❋ Look at two groups of rats. How much would the people have to pay if the piper asked for a dime for each rat?

4 Encourage children to use the groups of rats on the page to make up their own questions for the class to figure out.

Here's More:

Use the reproducible of 100 rats to answer more complex money questions. You might use overhead play money and ask volunteers to show the class how to figure out amounts such as these:

❋ If the piper wants a penny for each rat, how much will the town have to pay?

❋ If these 100 rats cost the town $1.00, how much would 200 rats cost?

❋ If 100 rats cost $1.00, how many rats would cost $3.00?

❋ If 100 rats cost $1.00, how much would 50 rats cost?

Assessment Ideas

Were children able to count to 100? Which children used groups of 10 to count to 100? Note which children were able to count in the abstract and which children used the money manipulatives to answer the questions.

MATH ACTIVITY CENTER Counting Coins

Provide play money and small classroom items tagged with prices. Encourage children to put out and then record the different coins they could use to pay for each item.

Literature Links

More about money can be found in Tana Hoban's *26 Letters and 99 Cents* (Greenwillow, 1987) and in Betsy and Giulio Maestro's *Dollars and Cents for Harriet: A Money Concept Book* (Crown, 1988).

Paying the Piper

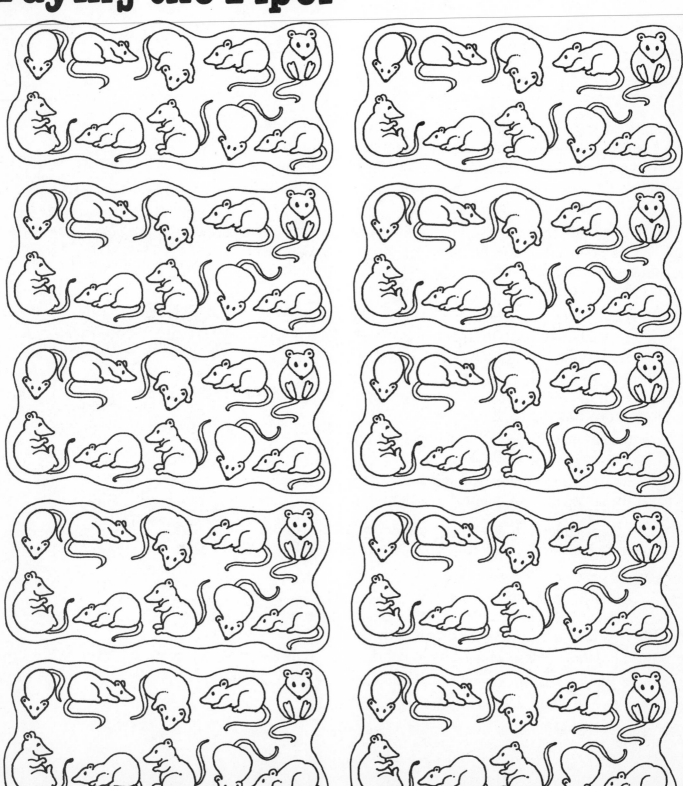

Money for the Piper

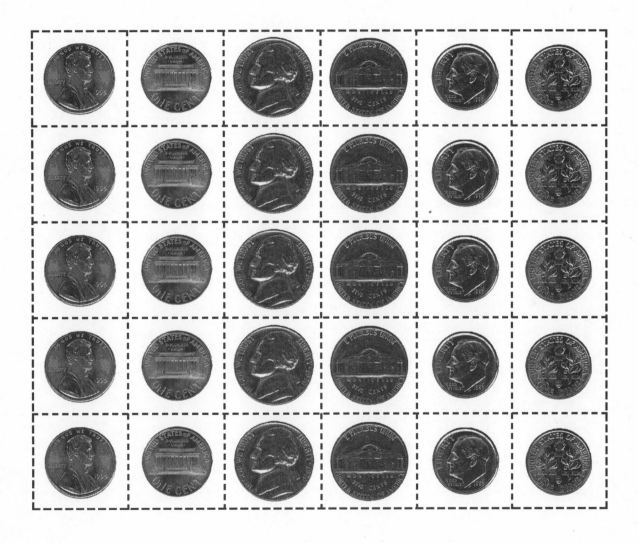

HICKORY DICKORY MATH   SCHOLASTIC PROFESSIONAL BOOKS

Name _____

My Math Journal